THE ABCs
OF FRIENDSHIP

By Edward Cunningham

Illustrated by

Valerie Hubbard Damon

👑 Hallmark Editions

INTRODUCTION

Friends are the ABCs
    in the alphabet soup of life.
They all look,
    sound and act differently
    from one another.
Yet each is important
    in a special way.
Here are some delightful glimpses
    into the world we share
    with those warm, whimsical,
    wonderful characters called friends.

Welcome to the ABCs of Friendship!

C is for COOKIES

Cookies and friends—
    they come in all shapes,
    colors and sizes.
Some are soft and sugarcoated,
    some are snappy and full of ginger
    and some are just plain nutty.
We can treat ourselves
    to many different kinds…

and there's always room for one more!

B is for BOOKS

Friends are like books on a shelf.

    They can be funny or serious.

    They can be popular

    or very hard to read.

But most of them

    have something interesting to say…

and every page

    brings a new surprise!

A is for ANGELS

Angels are perfect,
    but most friends aren't angels.
Most friends are people.
    Of course, some people are angels,
but usually no one we know,
    which is a good thing…

because friends
    are lots more fun than angels!

D is for DANDELIONS and DAISIES

Friends can pop up anywhere.
    They can be a nuisance one day
    and a joy the next.
And they can be cultivated
    anytime of year.
    As a wise old person once said…

"Friends are the brightest blossoms
    in the flowerpot of life!"

E is for ELEPHANTS

Elephants are famous
    for having big hearts
    and thick skins.
They never forget a favor
    or a kindness.
Good friends are twice
    as thoughtful as elephants…

but only about half as nosey!

F is for FASHIONS

Fads and fancies
   change with the seasons,
but the best friendships
   are the ones
   we're most comfortable with.
They wear well,
   keep their shape...

and never go out of style!

G is for GOLD

Many of life's treasures
    are here today
    and gone tomorrow.
But the gold of friendship
    is a magic thing…

the more we spend it
    on each other,
the richer we become!

H is for HOUSES

Real friends never care
  whether we live in cottages
  or in castles
as long as our welcome mats
  are out…

and we do our best
  to make them feel at home!

I is for ISLANDS

Think of islands in the middle
 of the sea.
 Sometimes people can be
 just as lonely
 and hard to reach.
But when we finally get there,
 we discover beautiful little worlds
 we never knew existed…

beautiful worlds of friendship!

J is for JEWELS

We all know people
    with lots of flash
    and very little worth.
They're just tricky imitations
    of the real thing…

but a true friend
    is a rare gem indeed!

K is for KALEIDOSCOPES

Friendship is full of surprises.
Just when we get used to looking at it
a certain way—
Presto!
we see a whole new design.
It might be a little more complicated
than the one we started out with…

but it's also a lot more beautiful!

L is for LEMONS

Sometimes a friend we thought was a peach
    turns out to be a lemon.
But sometimes we meet the kind of friend
    who is a blend
    of delightful ingredients—
    never too sweet, never too sour,
    always just right.
A friend like that
    is as refreshing as cold lemonade
    on a hot summer day.

Ah…friendship!

M is for MAPS

Life is an easy place to get lost in.
    Now and then
    it takes a friend
    to show us the way
    around the detours,
    over the rough spots
    and out of the woods....

Blessed are the pathfinders!

N is for NEWSPAPERS

Friends arrive in sections.
  Some are all business
  and others are full of gossip.
  Some are good sports
  and others are loaded with funnies.
They keep us in touch
  with what's going on in the world...

from the front-page headlines
  to the strictly personals!

O is for OAK TREES

Ever watch a friendship grow?
    It starts off as a tiny acorn,
    but with a little care
    and a lot of luck
    it can become a mighty oak.
This is a fascinating process…

but it never happens overnight!

P is for PEACOCKS, PENGUINS, PELICANS and PARRAKEETS

In any flock of friends,
    we'll meet the frumpy
    as well as the fine-feathered,
    the dazzling
    as well as the down-to-earth.
It's fun to know all kinds…

even the really weird ducks!

Q is for QUILTS

We may strike up
   comfy and cozy friendships,
   or colorful and crazy ones.
But no matter what
   their patterns may be…

friendships are designed
   to keep us warm!

R is for RAINBOWS

Rainbows of friendship
    color our days
    with a happiness
    that never seems to fade.
They curve
    far beyond the horizon
    of here and now…

but the treasure is at *this* end!

S is for SMILES

Smiles are happy and fun
   and feel good
   and look nice
   and don't cost anything.

And nothing is friendlier
   than a great big smile!

T is for TELEVISION

Friendship tunes us in
    on a variety of programs.
It may be
    a situation comedy on Monday,
    an adventure movie on Wednesday
    and a soap opera by Friday.

Once in a while...
    it's a late-night talk show!

U is for UMBRELLAS

When skies look dark and scary
  and stormy weather is due,
  a trusty friend
  can really come in handy
to keep our spirits
  from getting soggy…

and to save us
  from catching "the lonelies!"

V is for VOLLEYBALL

The game of life
    is a thrill a minute.
Some days we win,
    and some days we lose.
    That's the way
    the ball bounces.
But even though
    we can't always
    predict the score…

it helps to have
    friendly teammates!

W is for WRISTWATCHES

Friends are all made differently.
   They can be rugged,
   shock-proof and self-winding,
   or they can be fragile,
   intricate and easy to shatter.
It's never easy to figure out
   what makes them tick…

but it's always worth the time!

X is for X RAYS

Wouldn't it be nice
   if we had a machine
   to look inside our friends
   and see when they are sad
   or worried,
   or in need of some help?
Sure it would,
   but since we don't…

there's no harm in asking!

Y is for YO-YO'S

Friendship has its ups and downs.
    Just as we get it spinning along
    free and easy—
    Whoops!
    it can start wobbling
    almost out of control.
Then Zip!
    it snaps right back
    where it started.
Being friends
    is one of life's
    most enjoyable pastimes…

and no one ever masters all the tricks!